Welcome to a world of limitless color and creativity!!!

This coloring book is more than just a set of pages to fill in—it's an open door to imagination and discovery! Whether you're a child seeking adventures or an adult searching for a moment of calm and escape, this book invites you to immerse yourself in a unique visual journey. Let your colors come to life as you explore magical landscapes, fantastic creatures, and captivating designs. Get ready to unleash your creativity, relax, and let your imagination soar with every stroke of color!

"May you find joy in every stroke of color, and may this book bring you peace and inspiration. Let it accompany you in moments of serenity and fuel your creative adventures!"

-IA

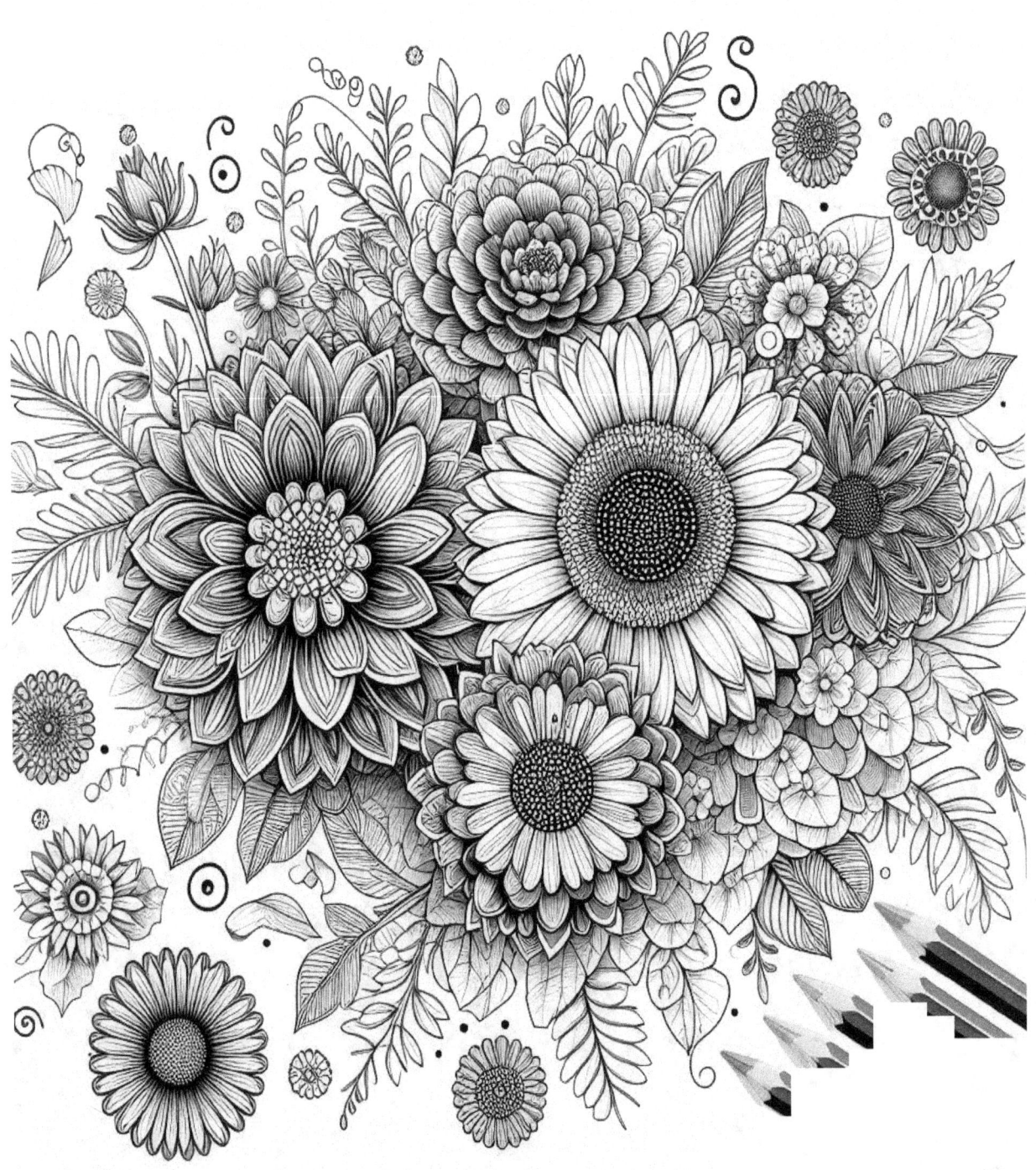

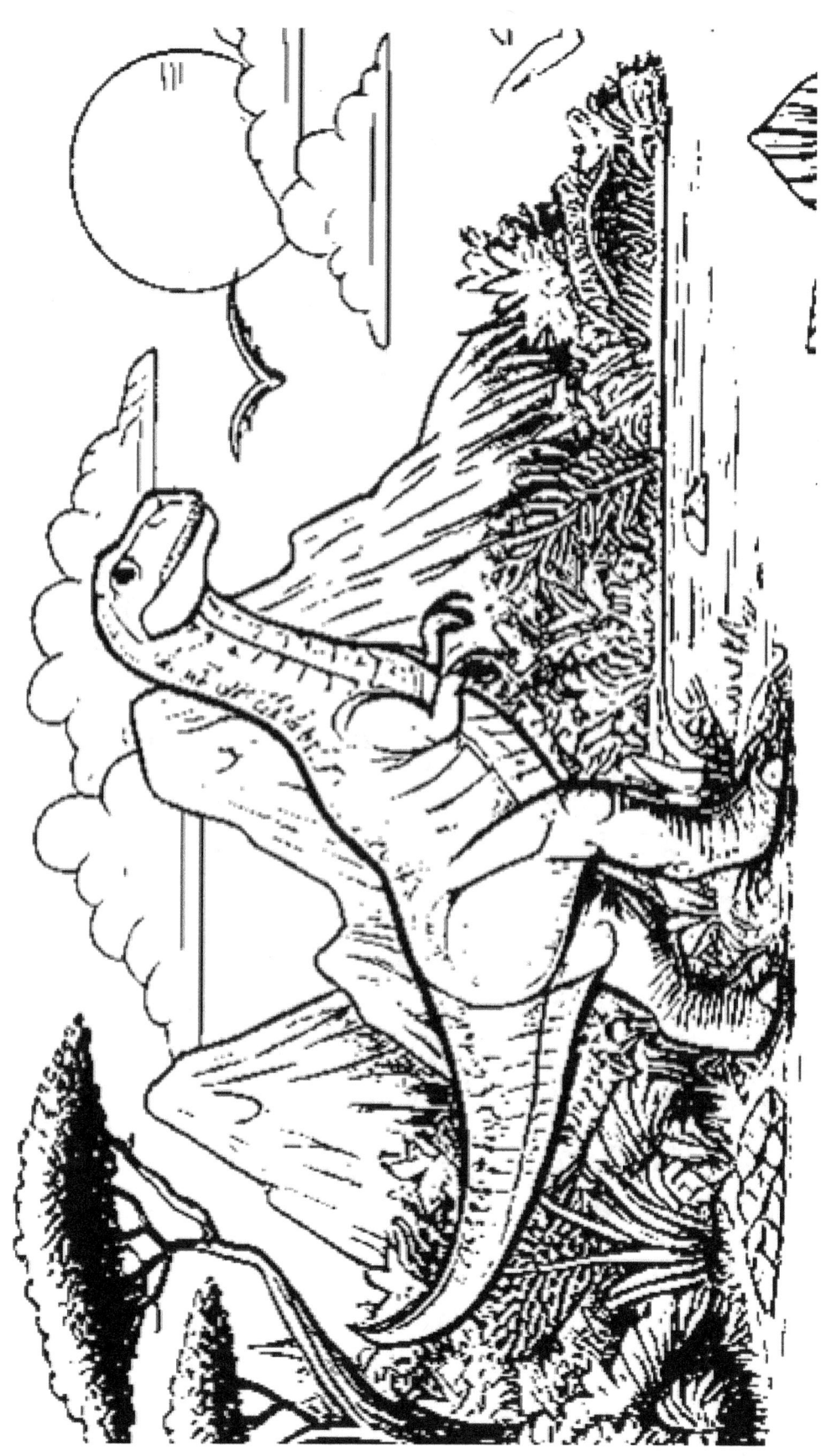

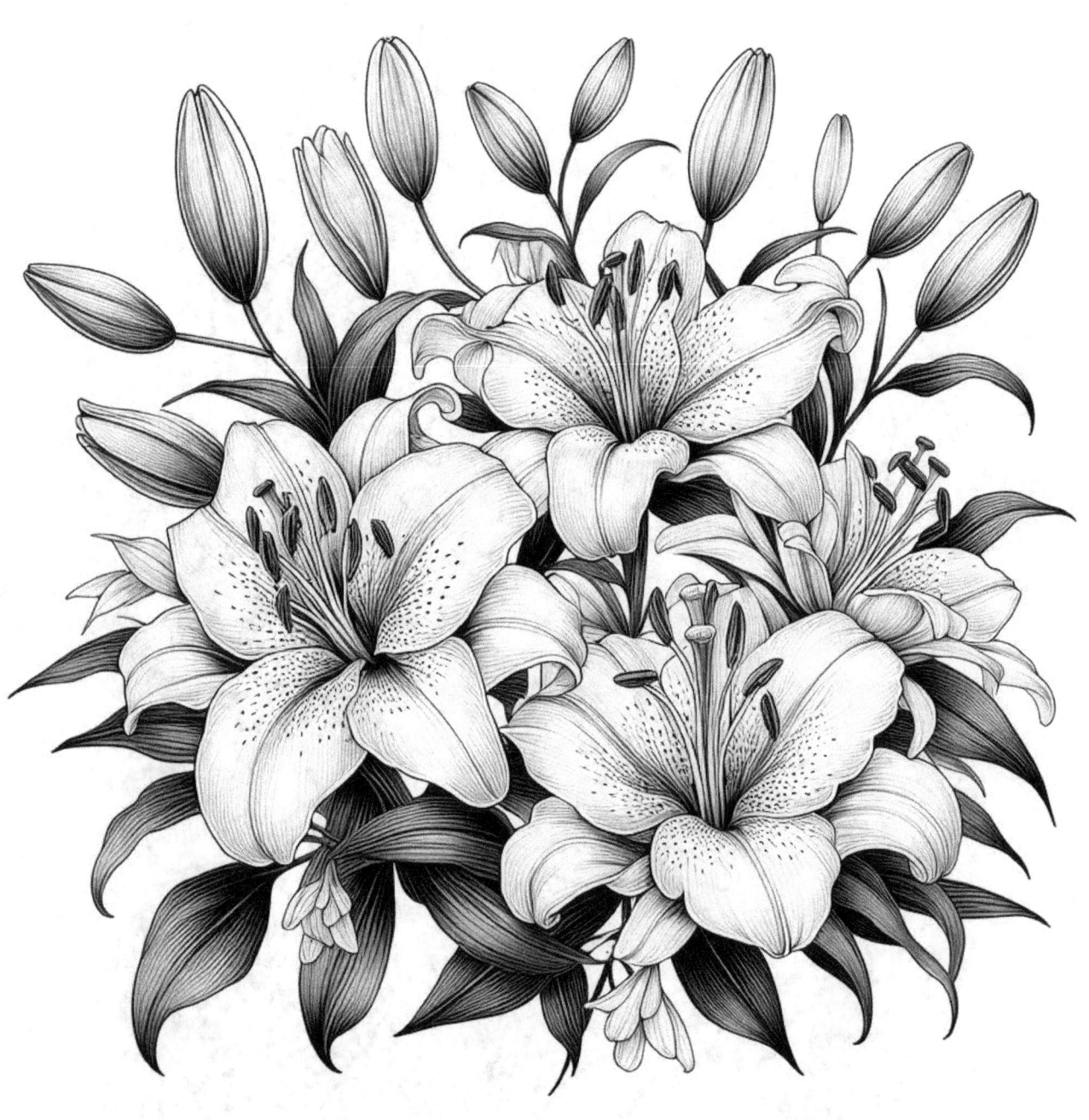

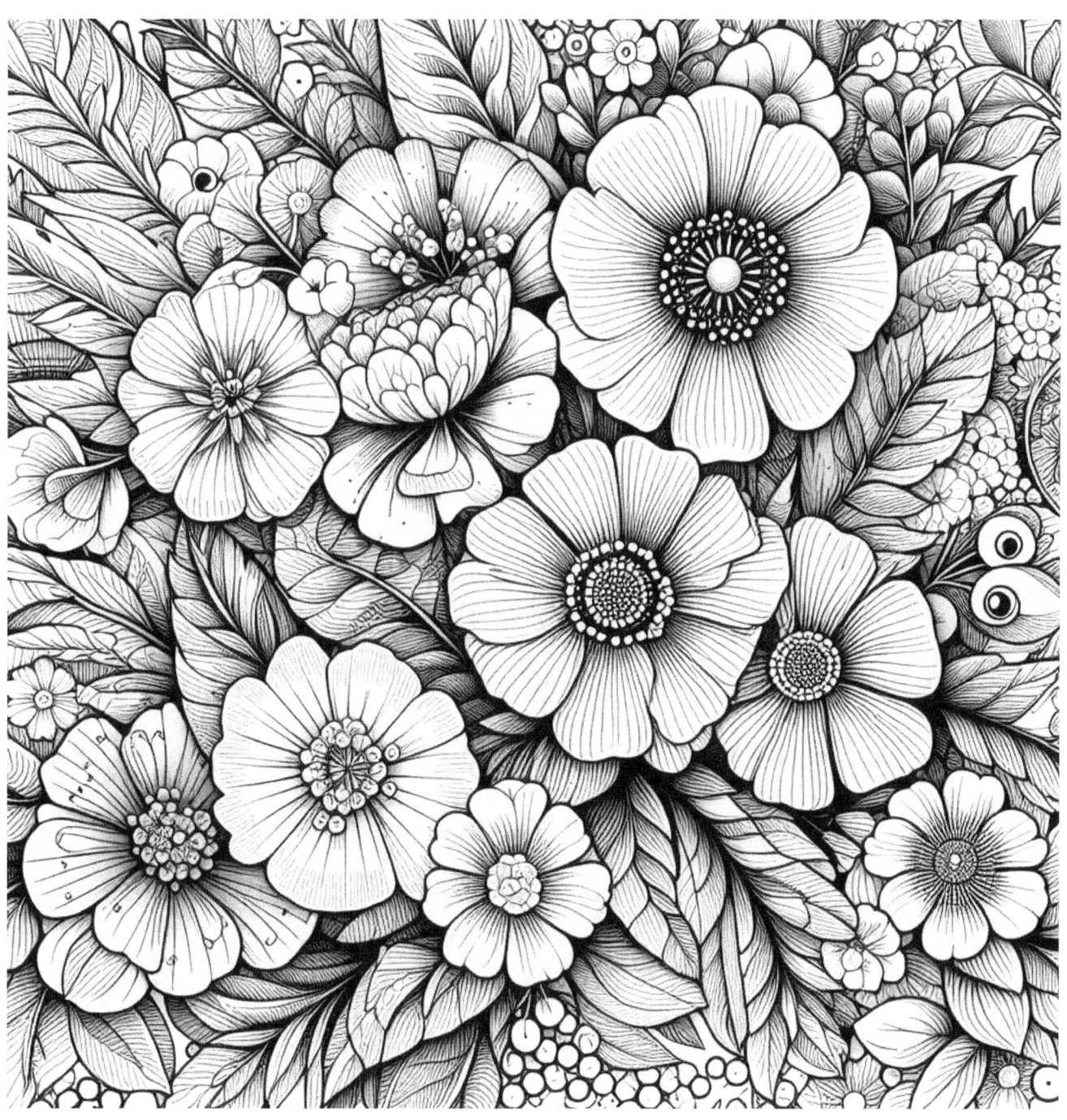

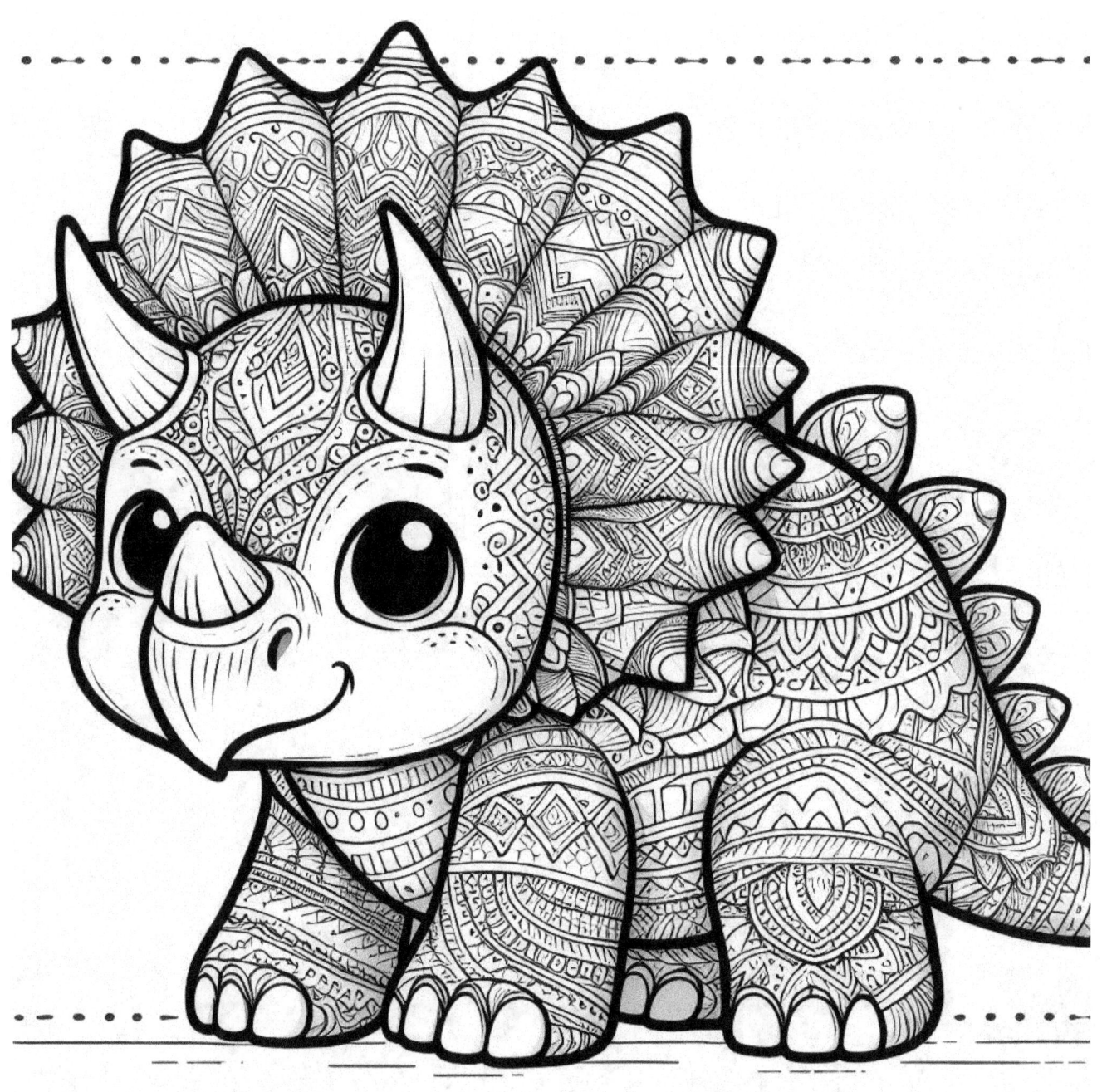

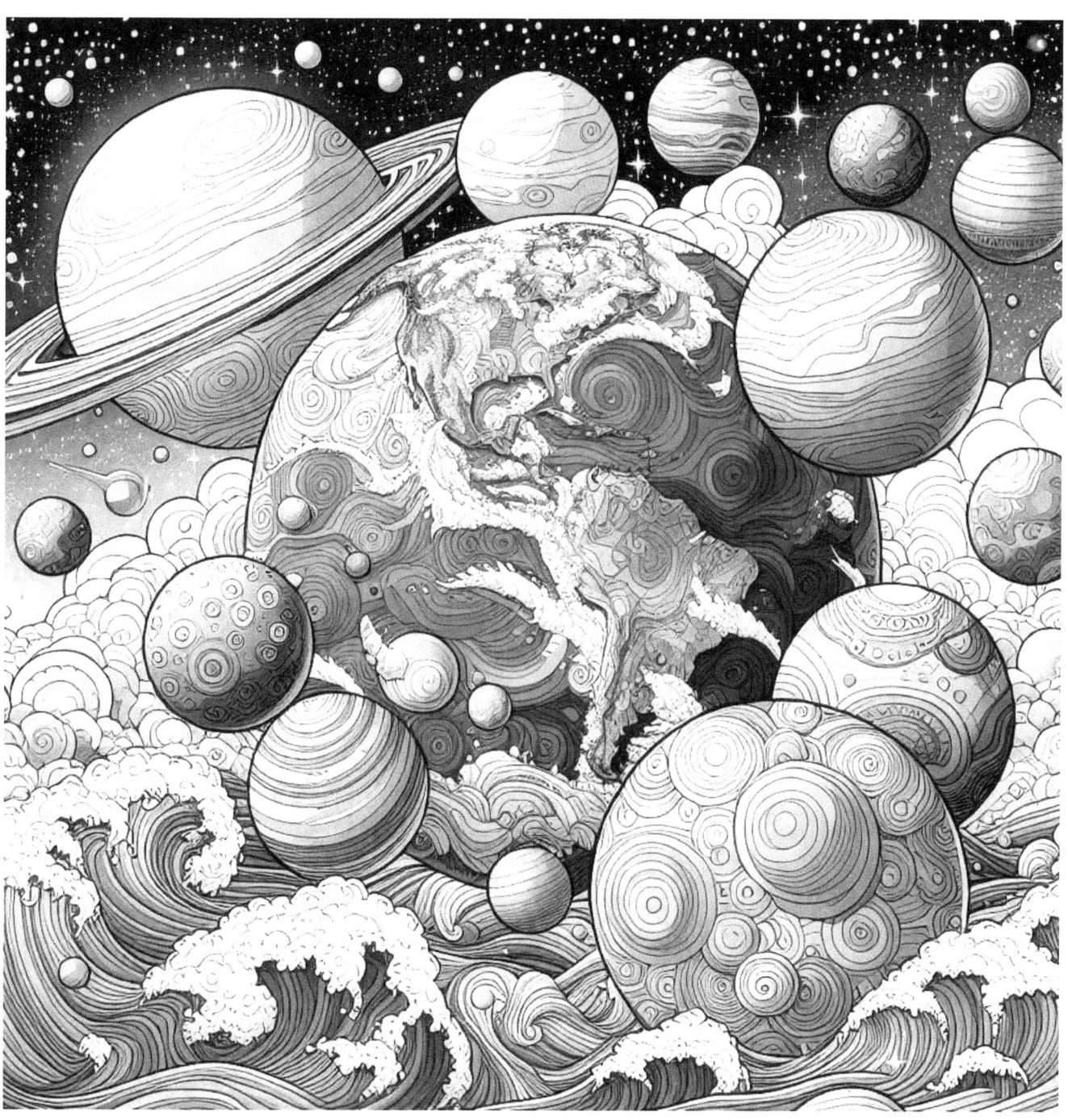

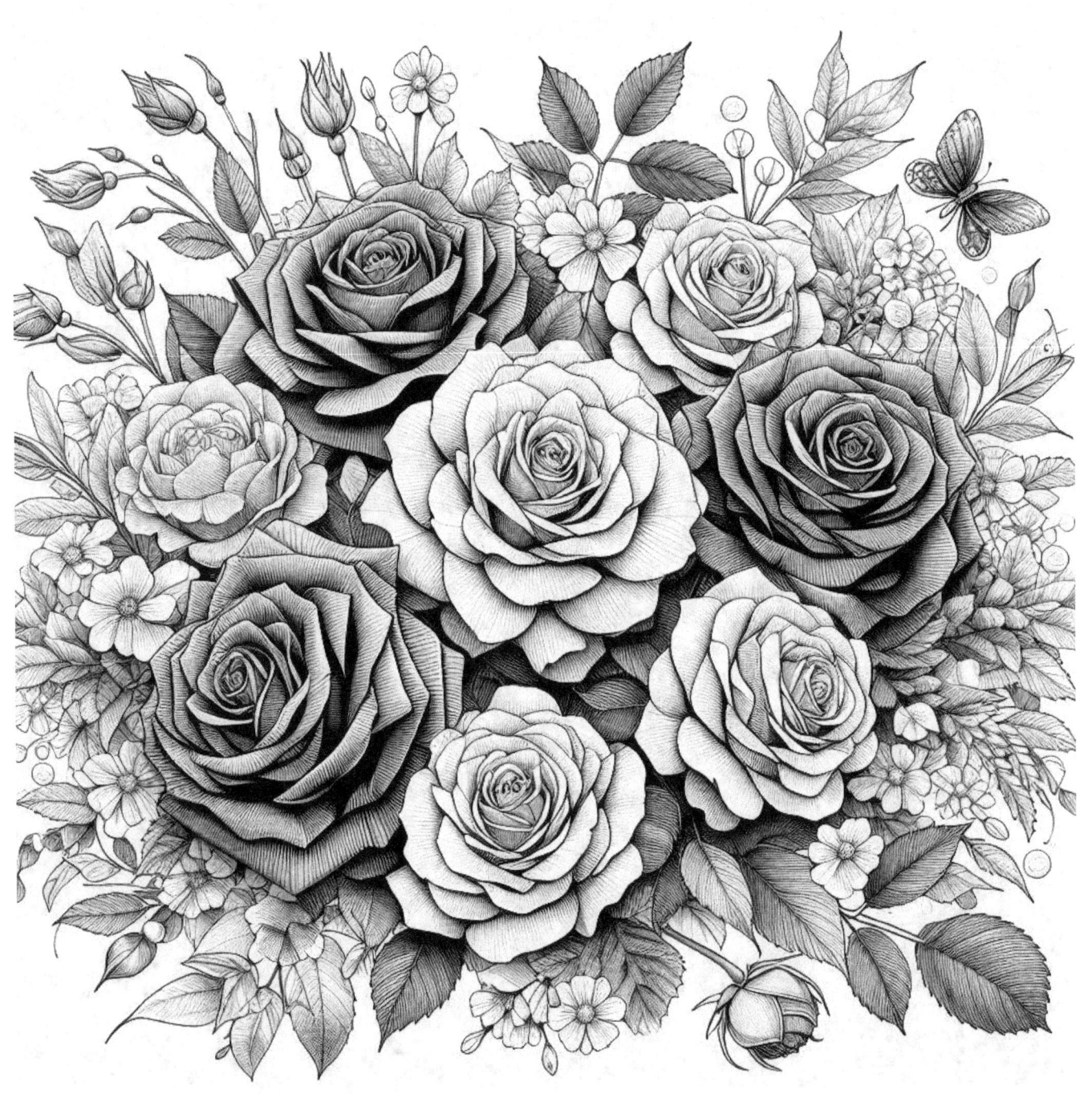

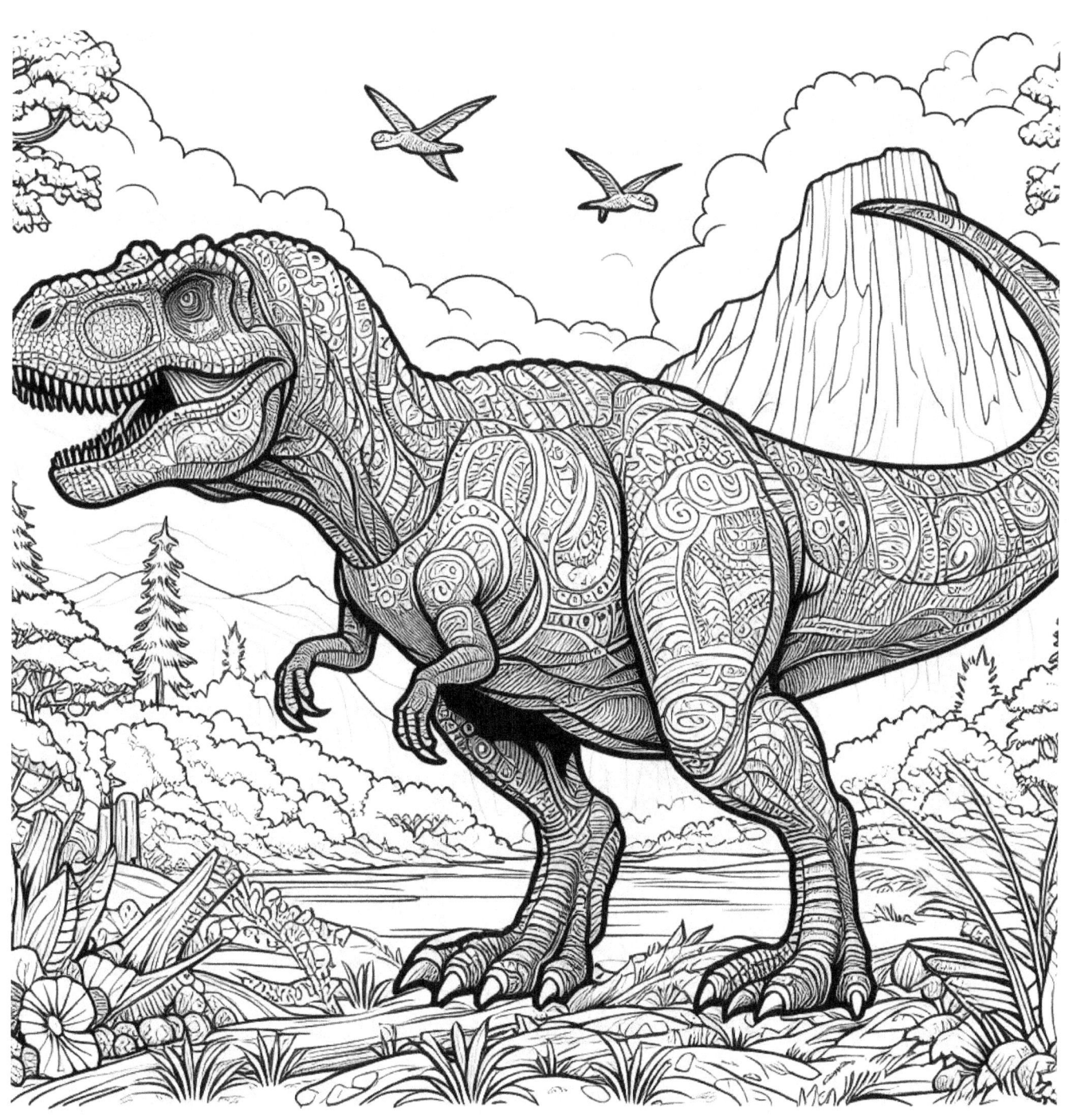

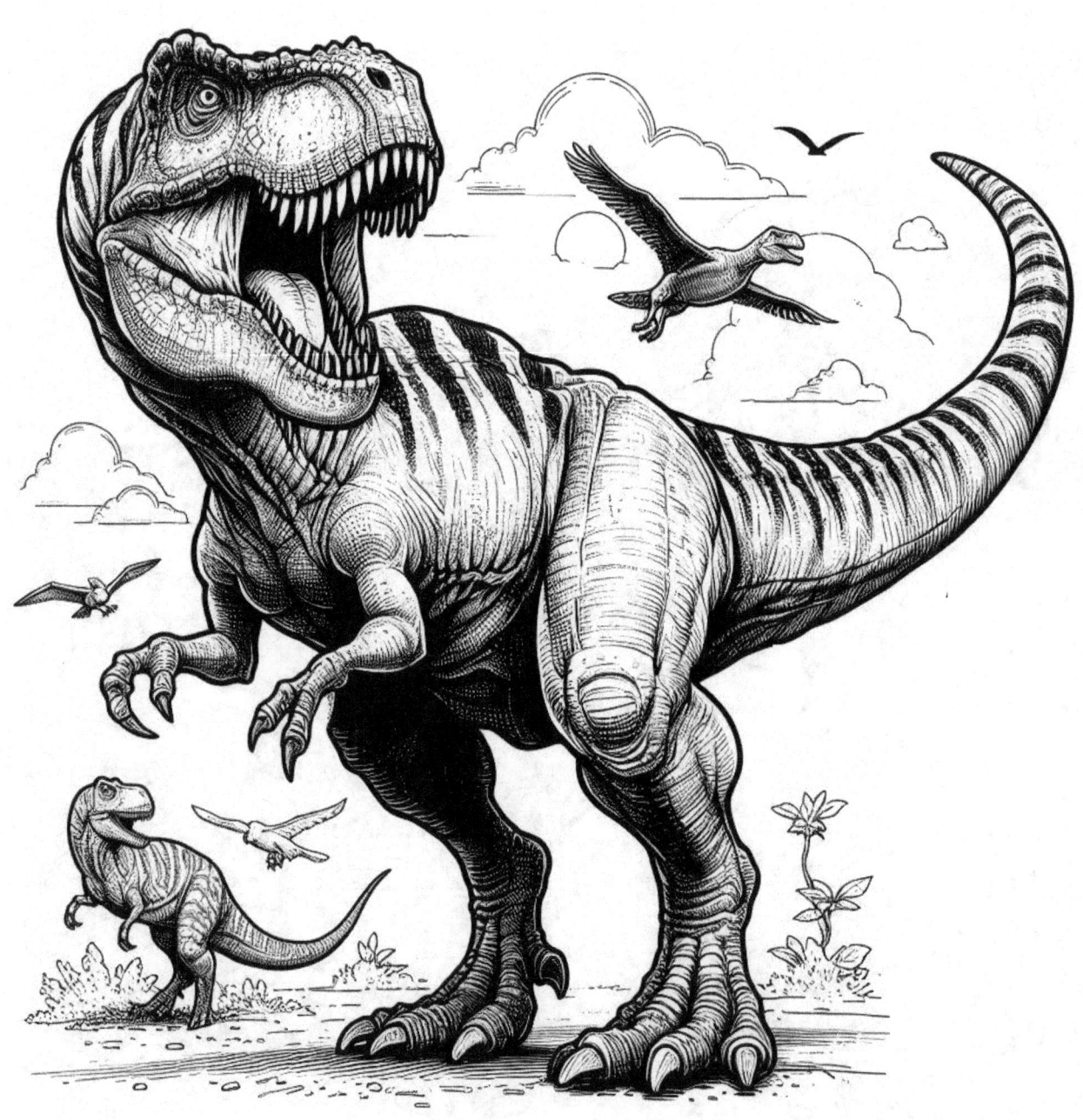

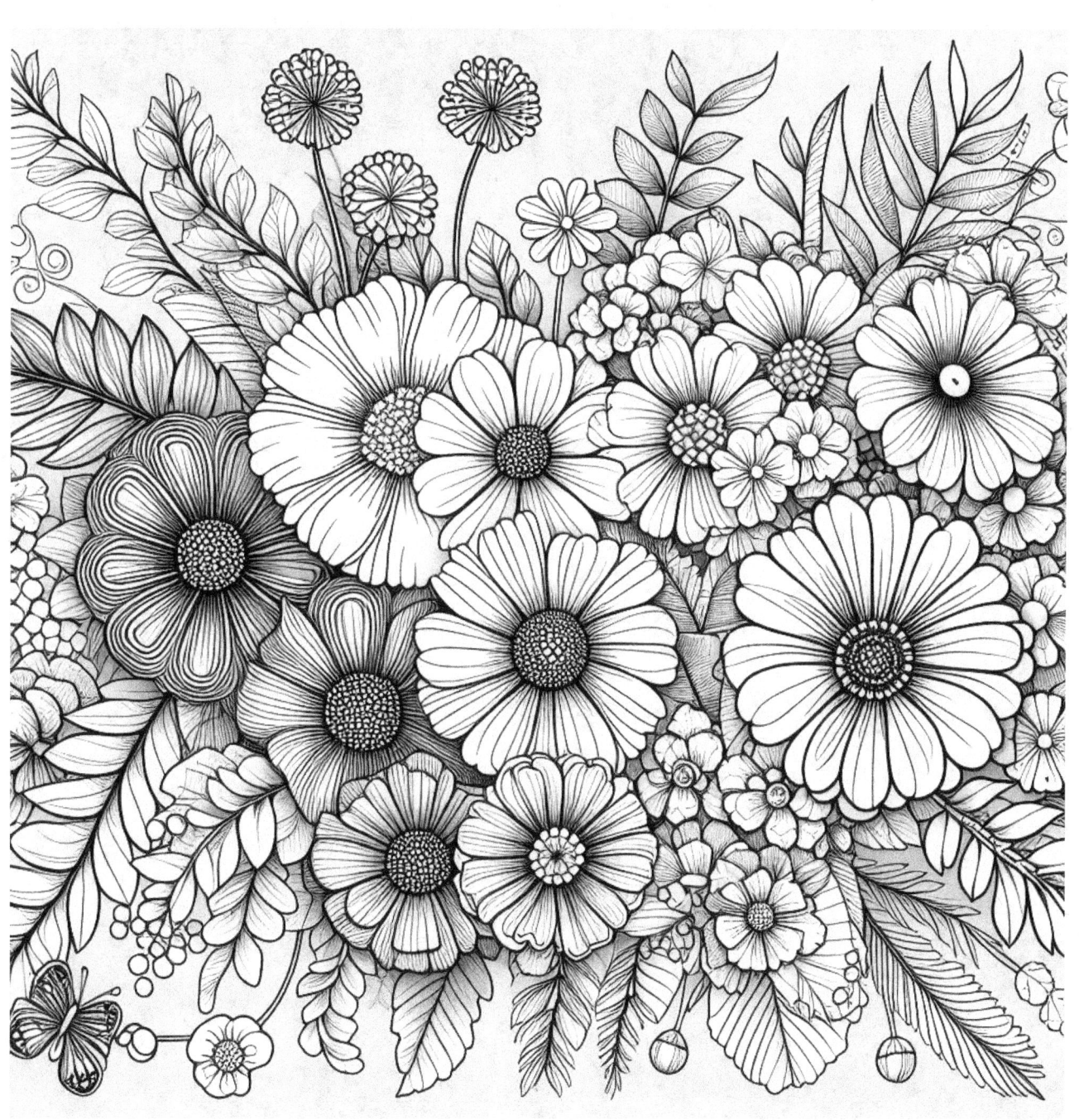

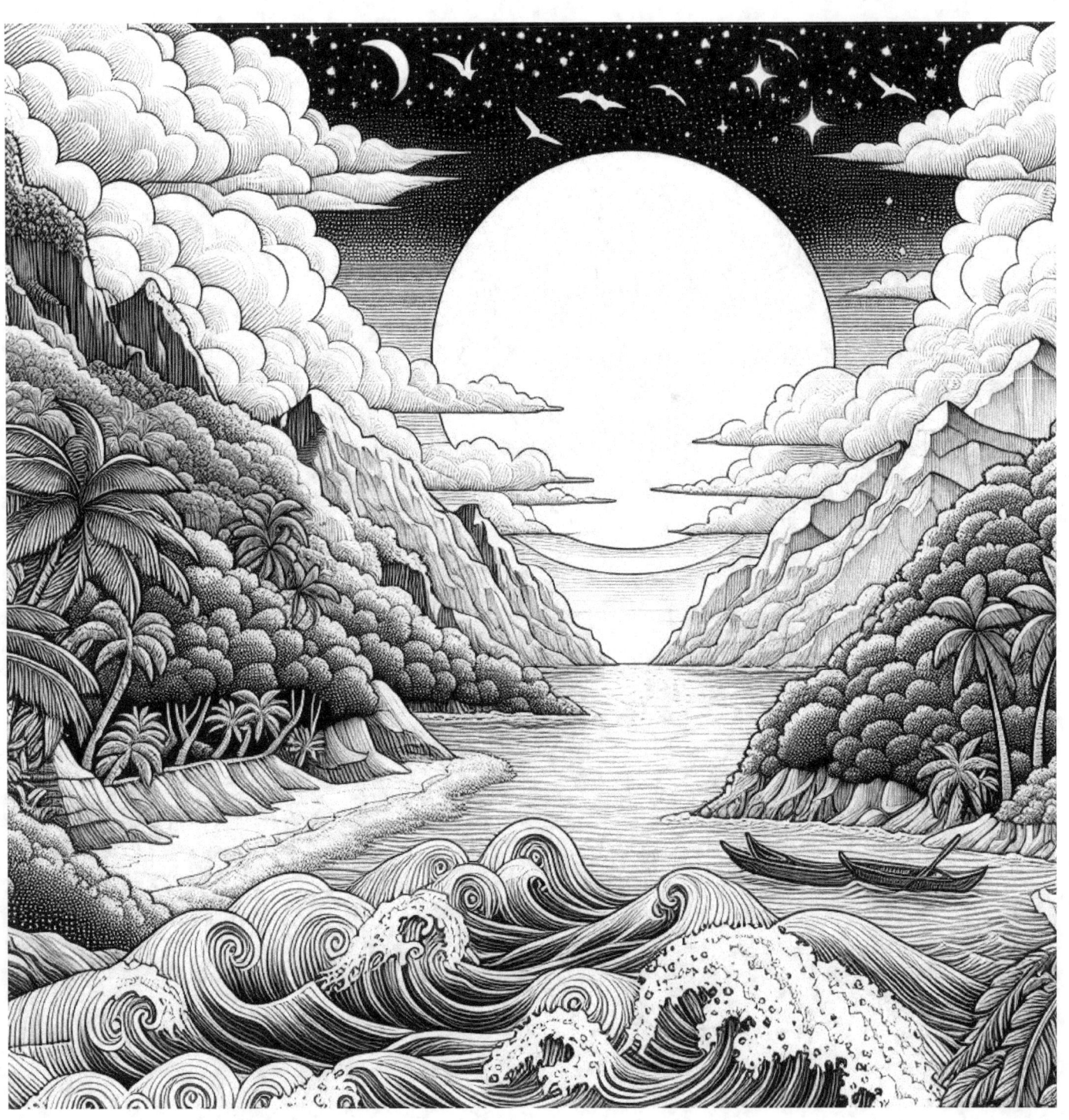

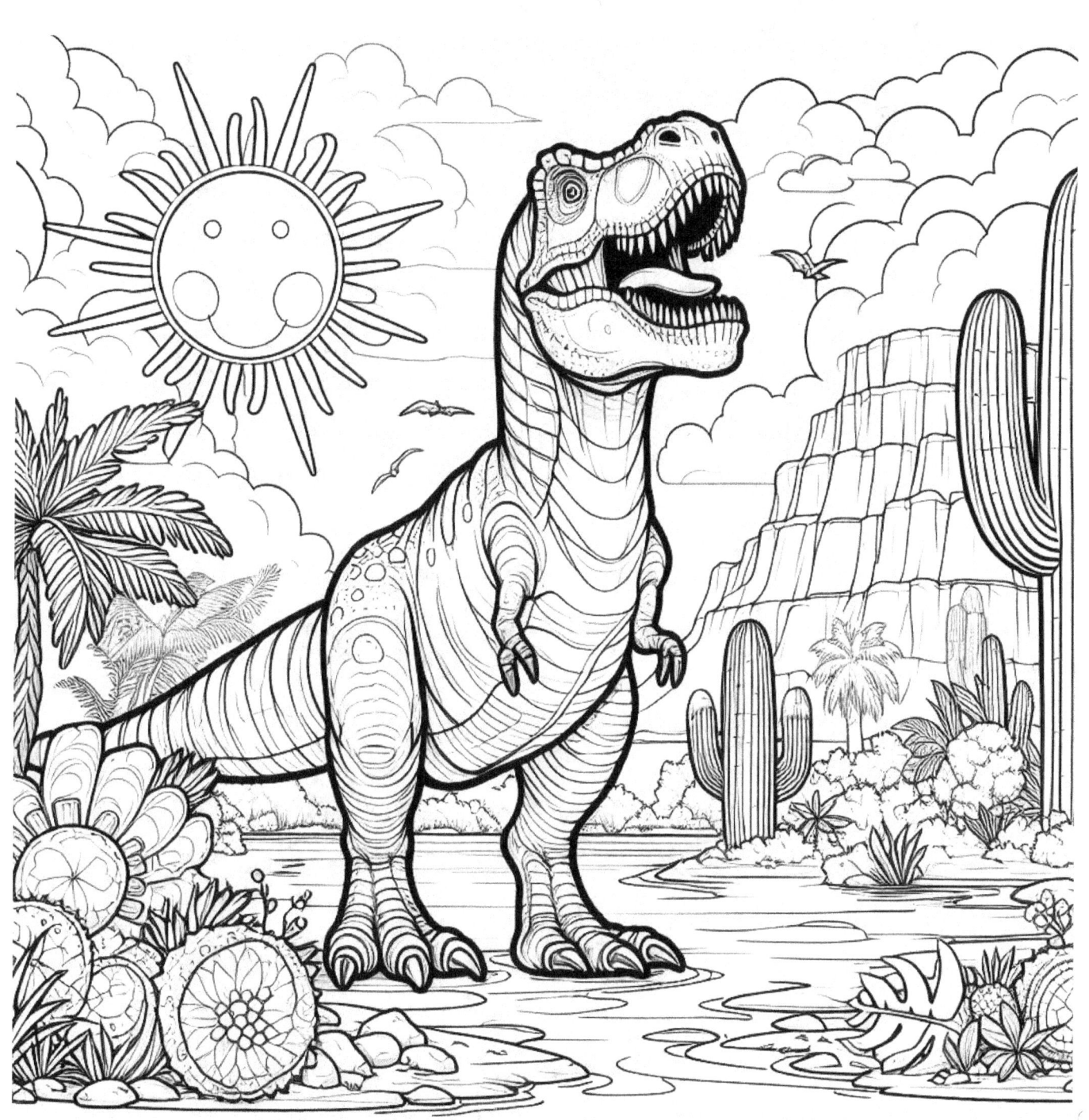

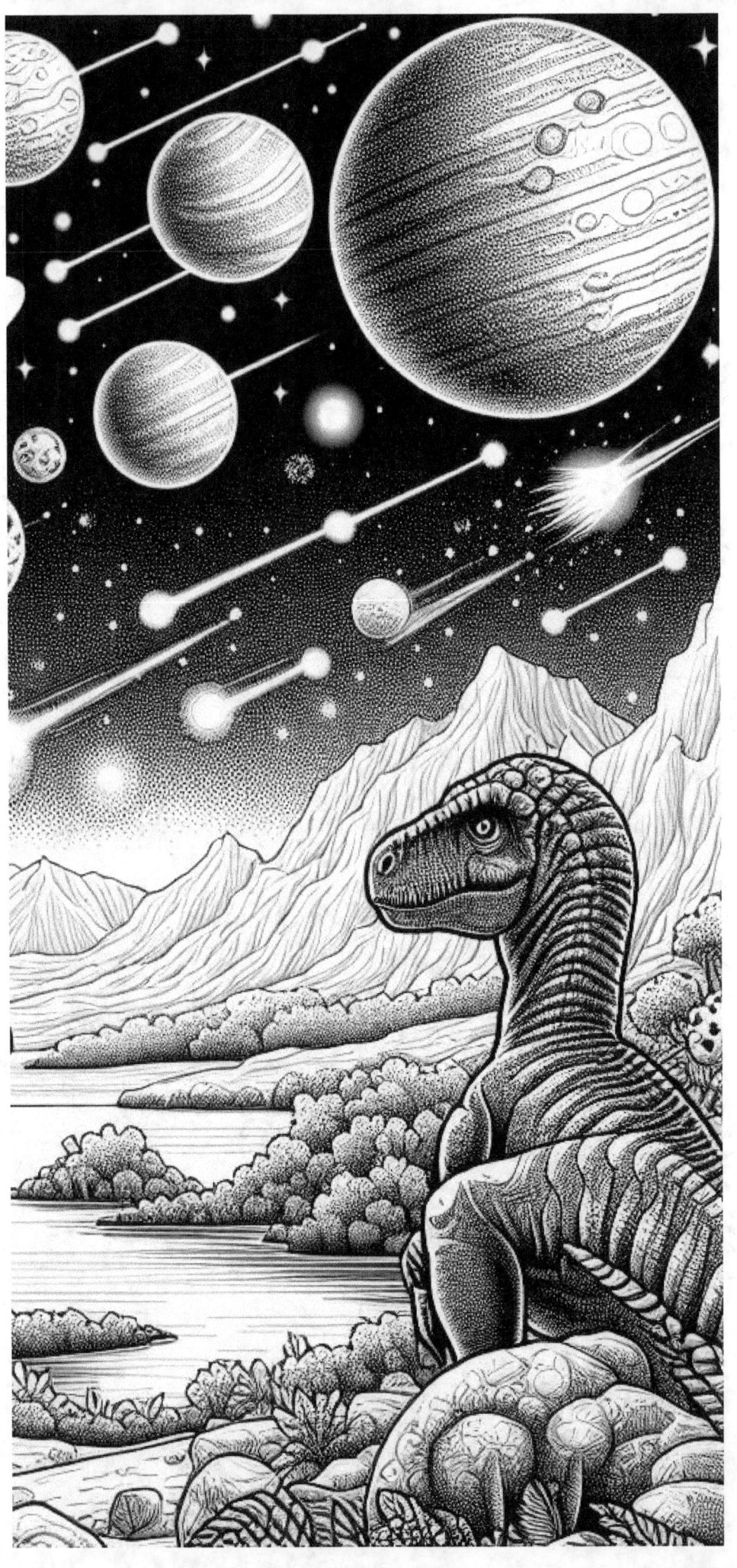

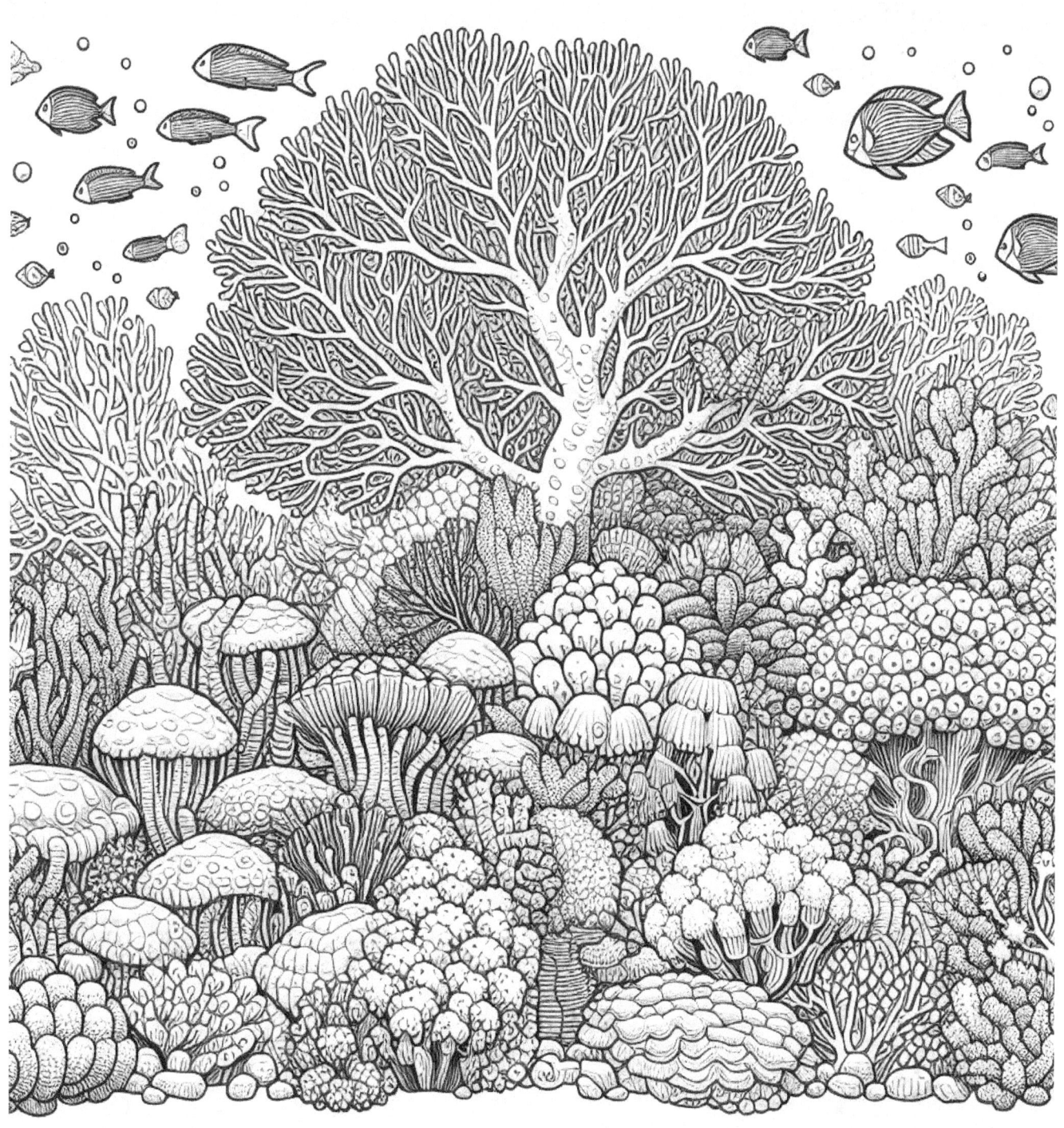

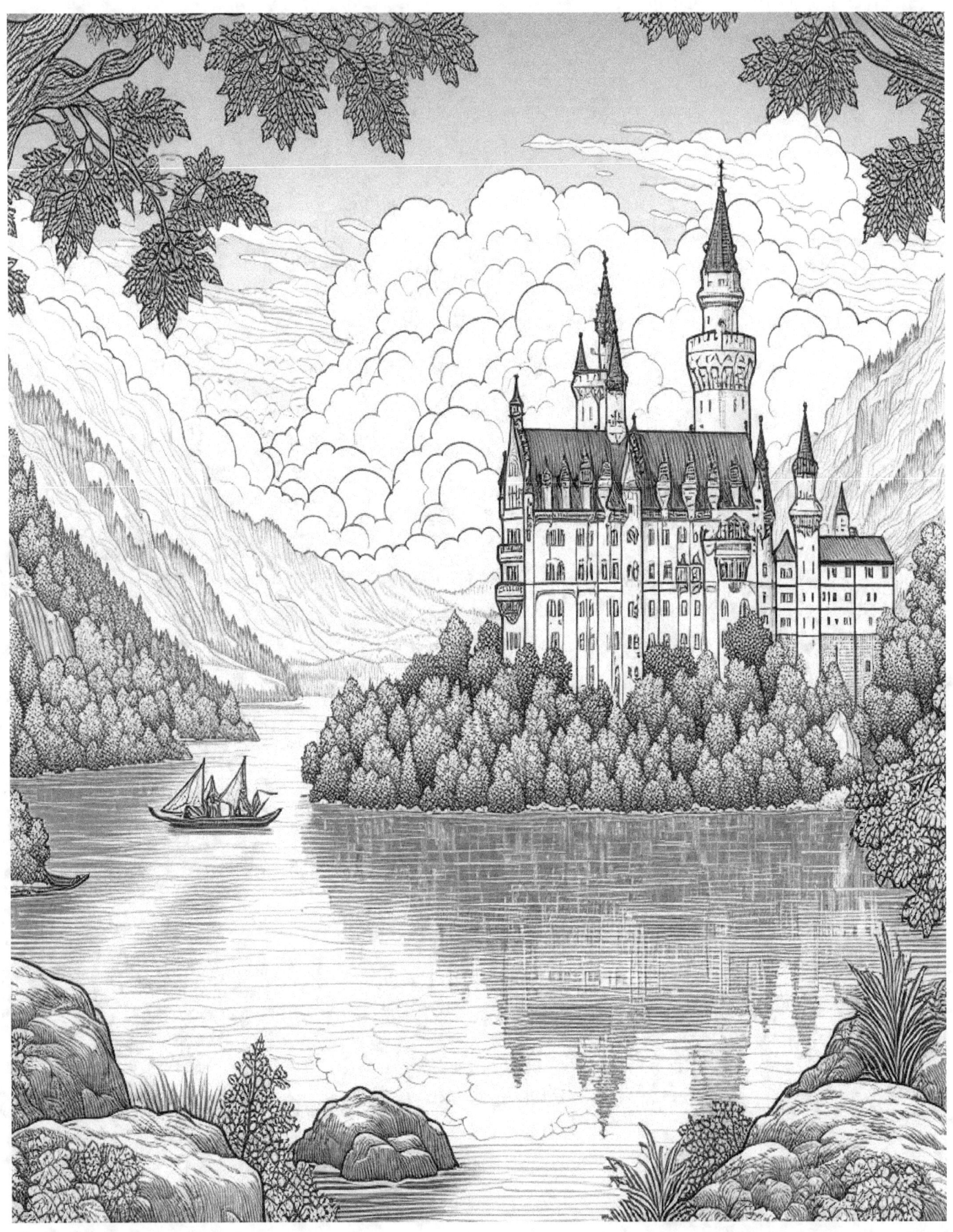

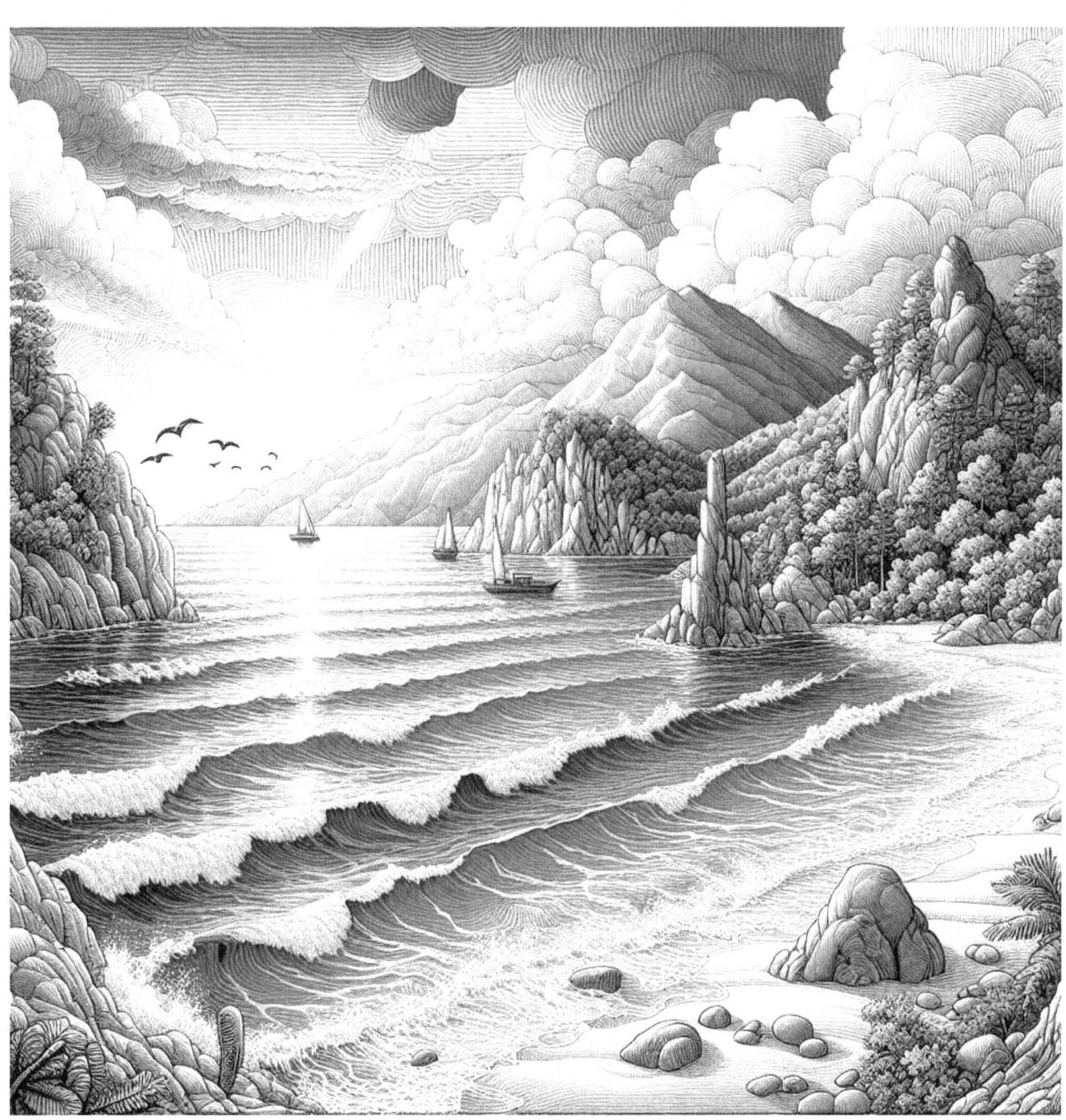

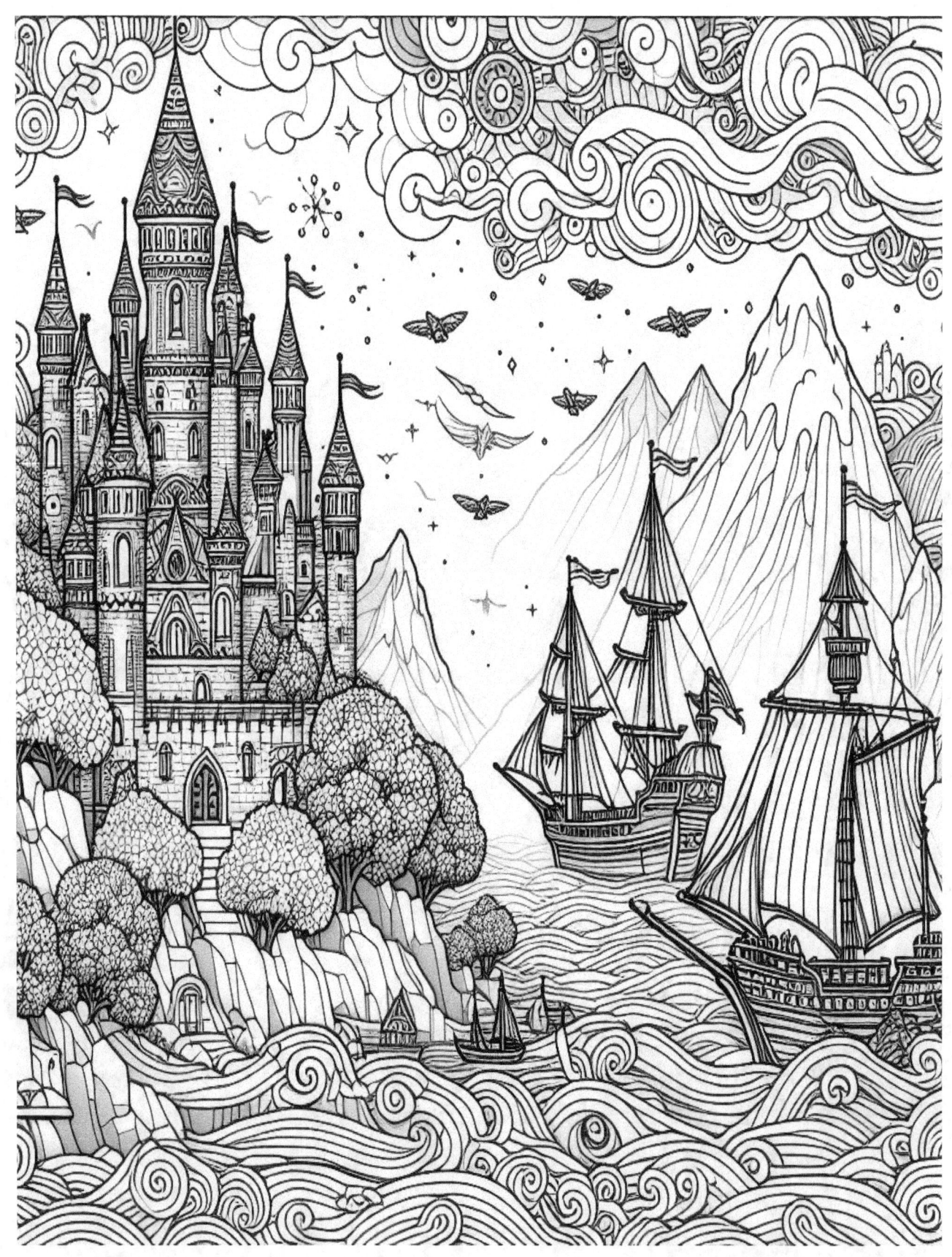

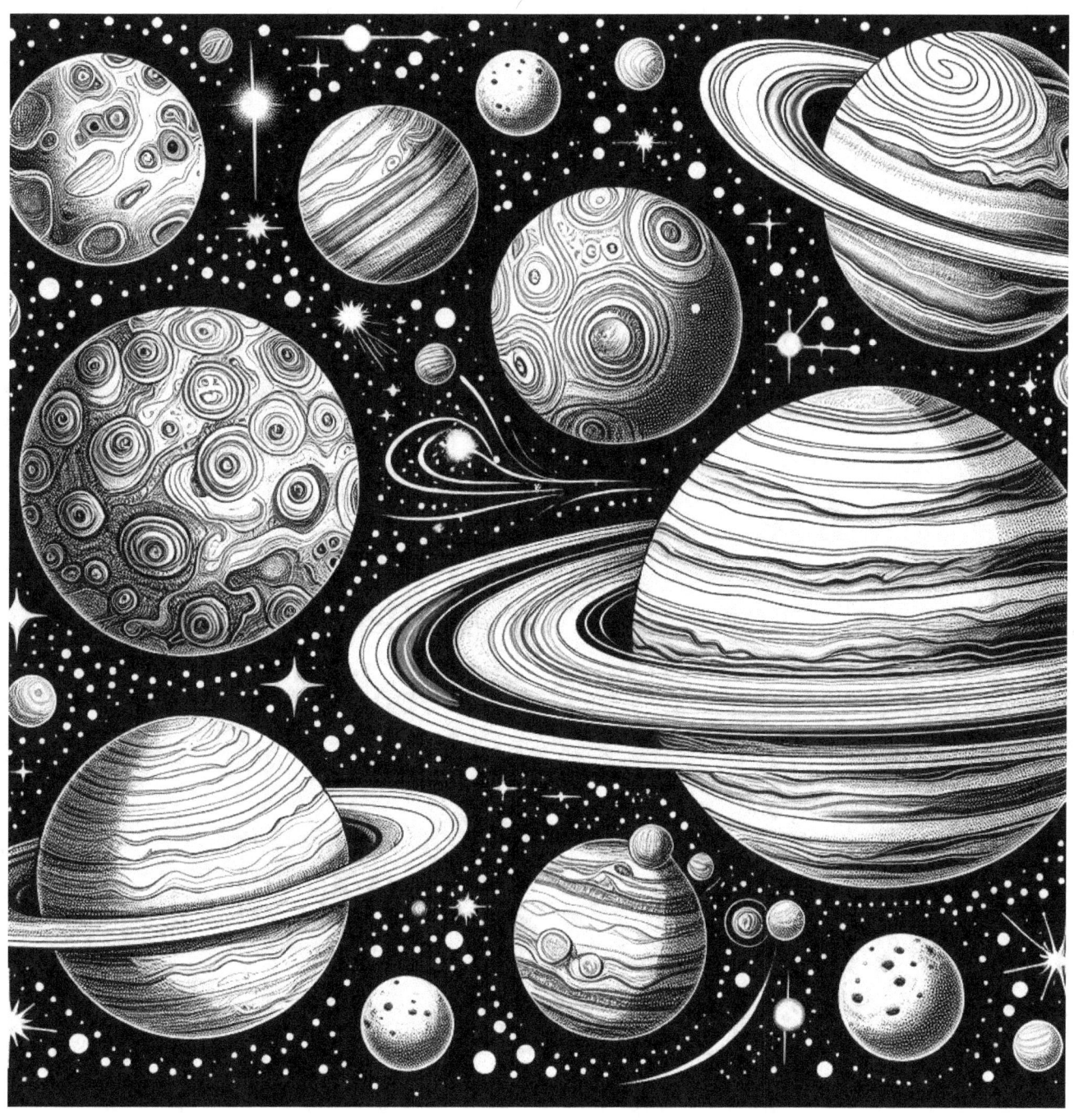

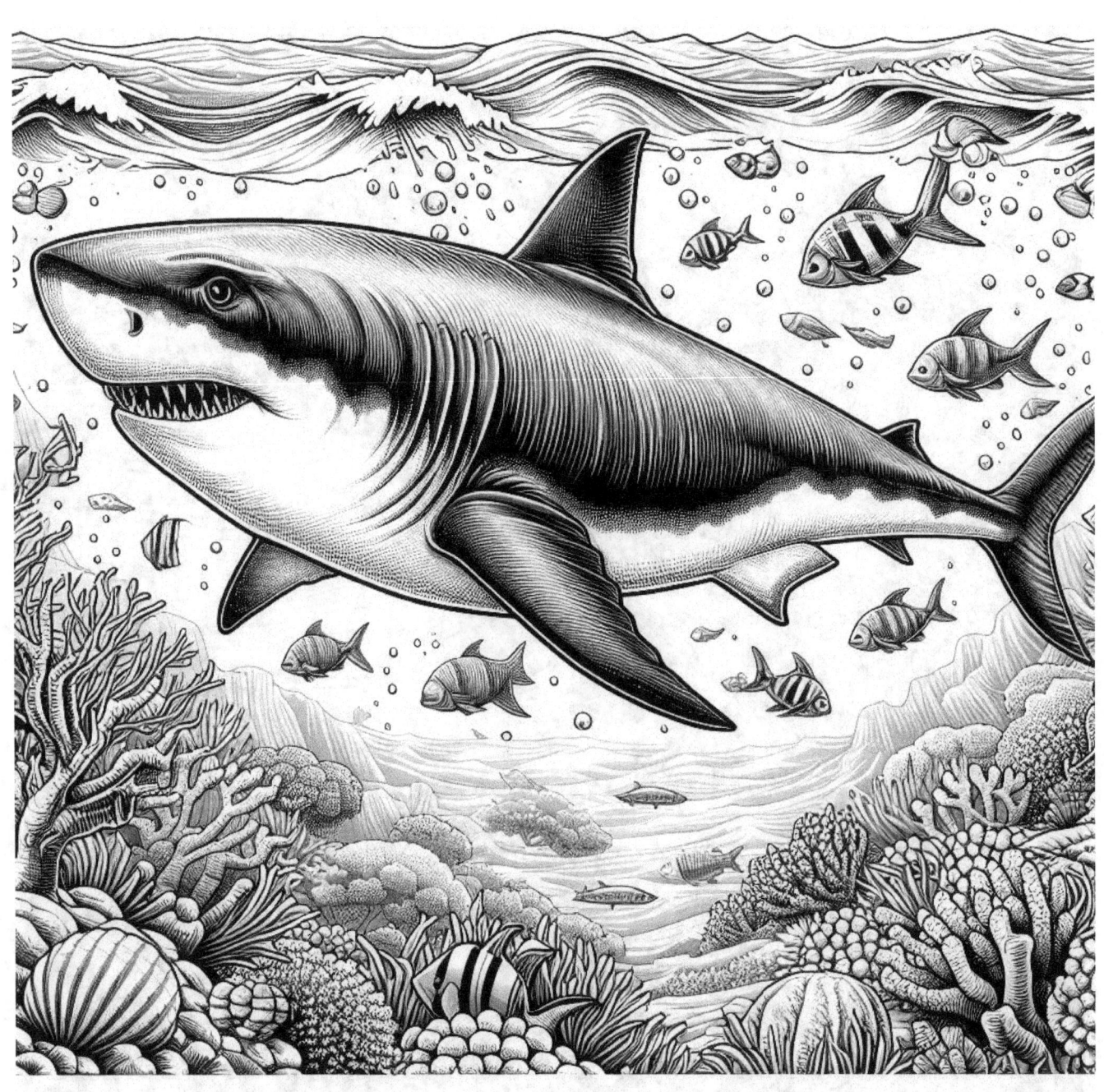

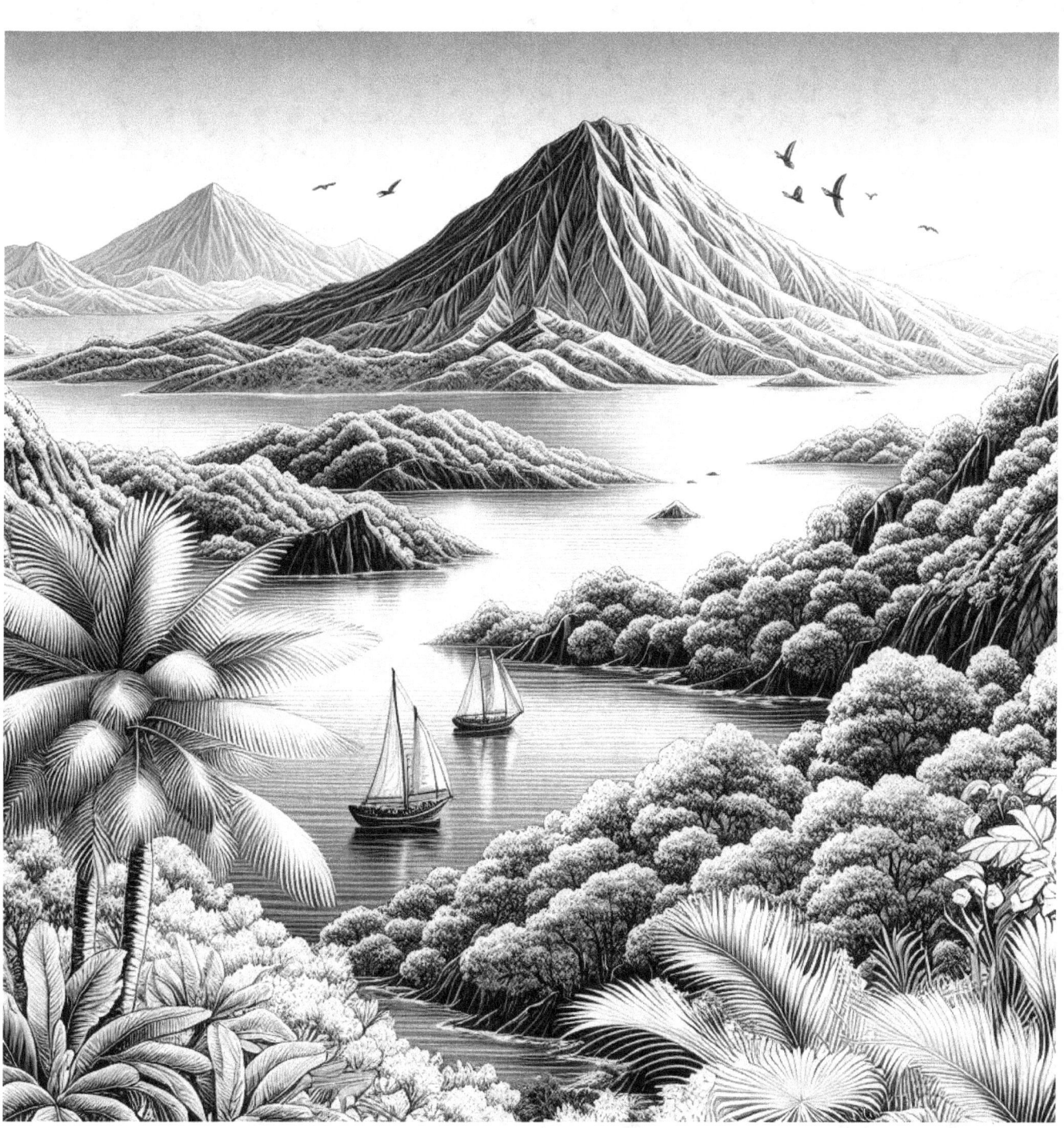

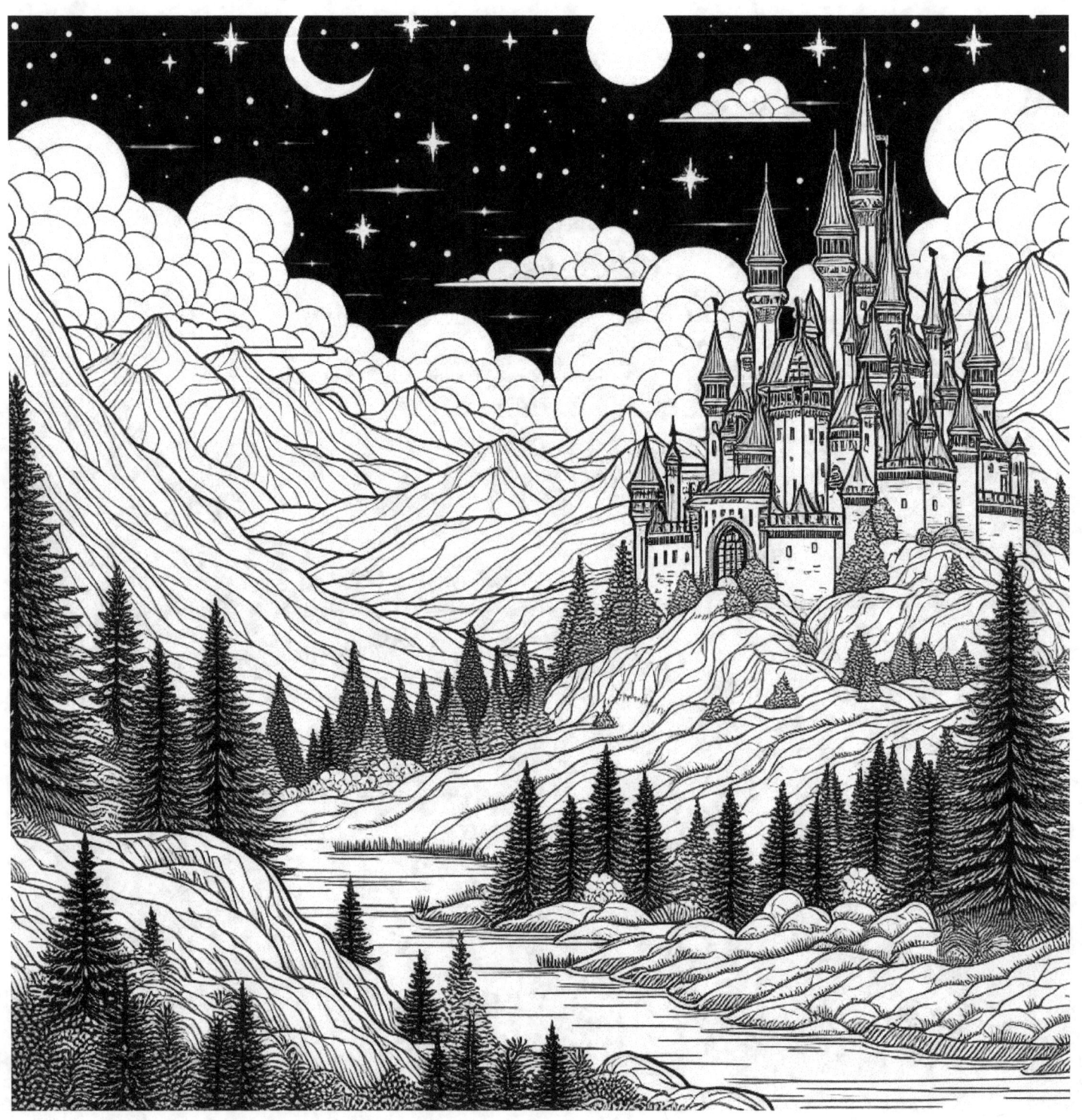

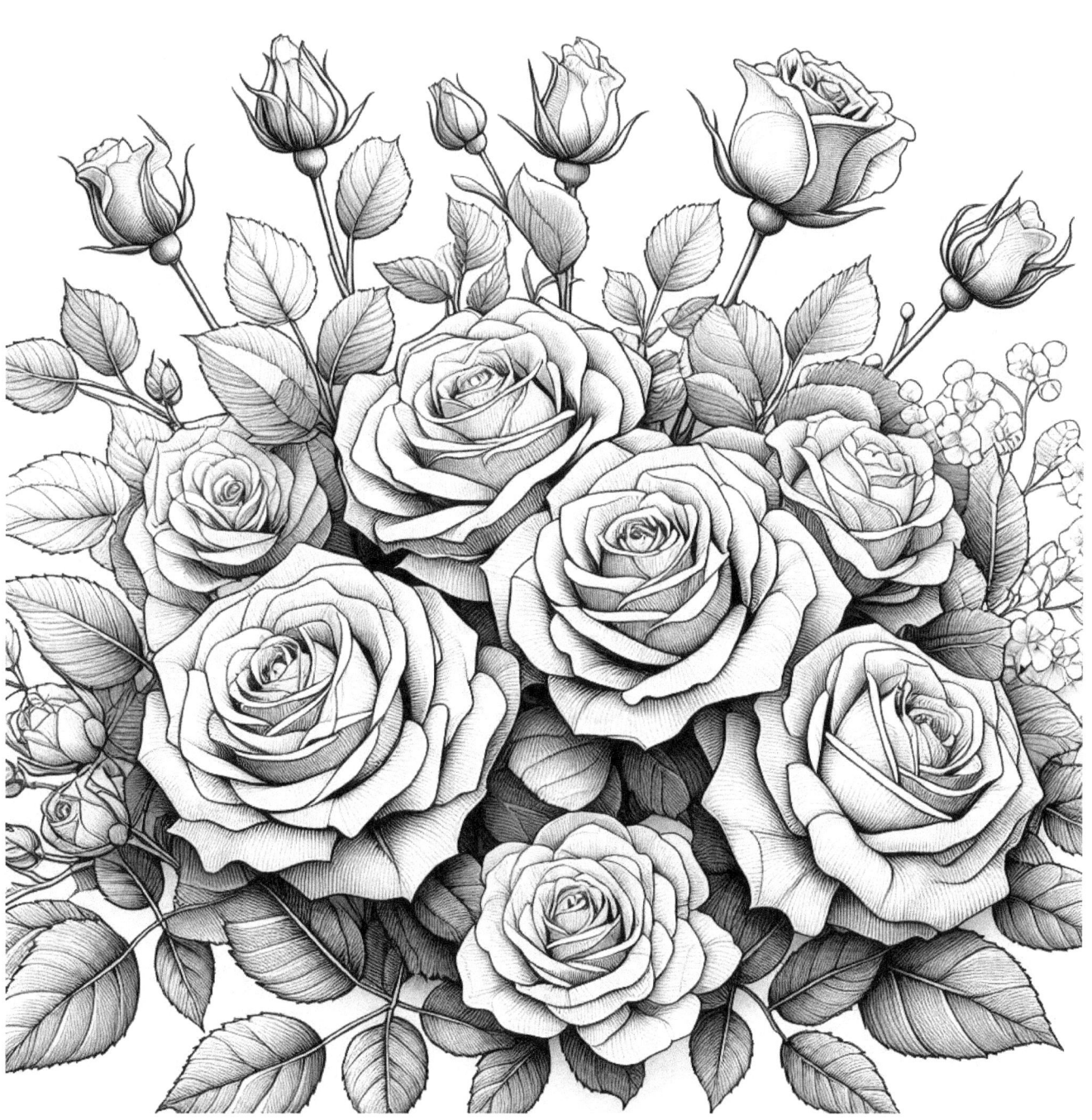

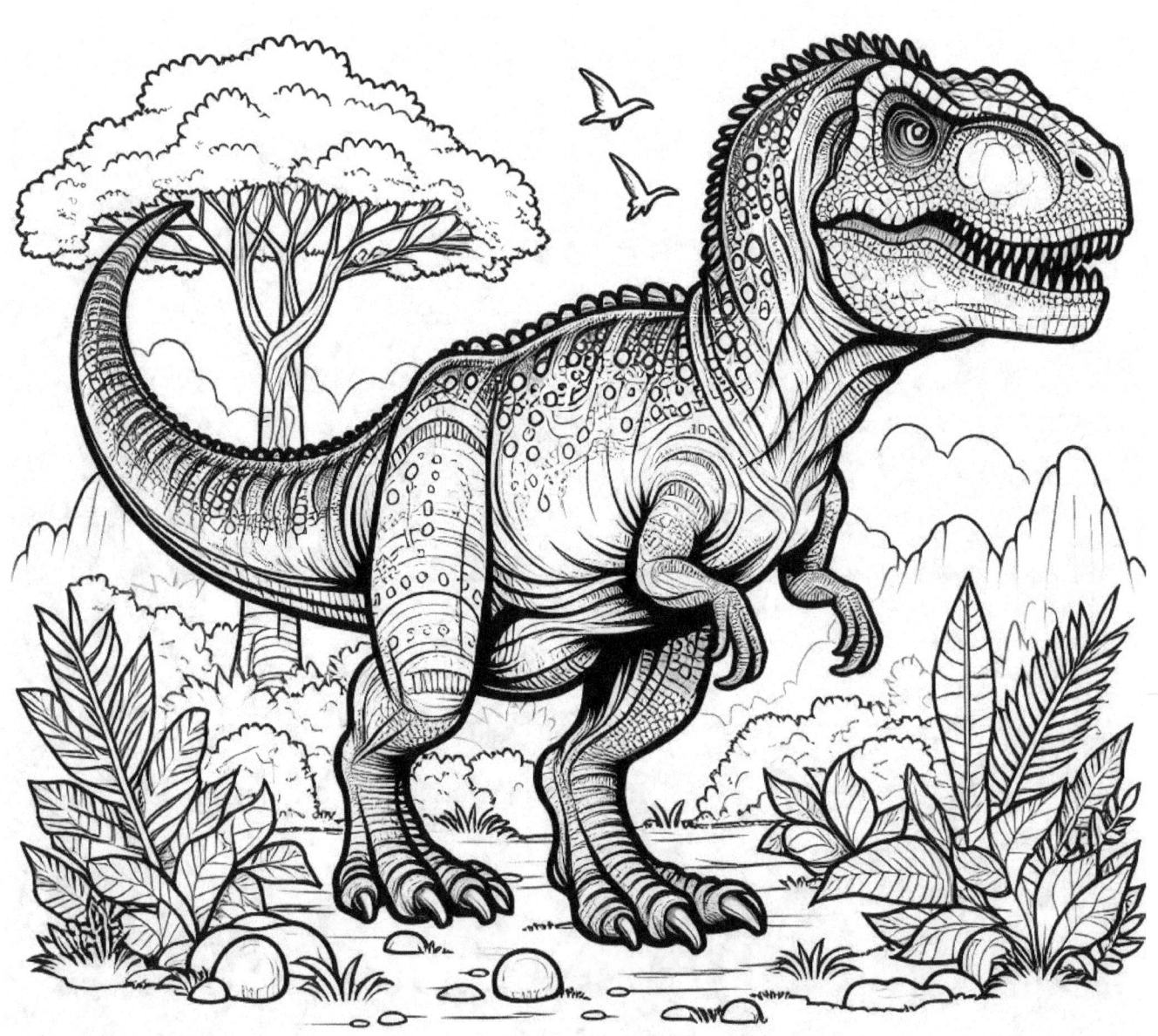

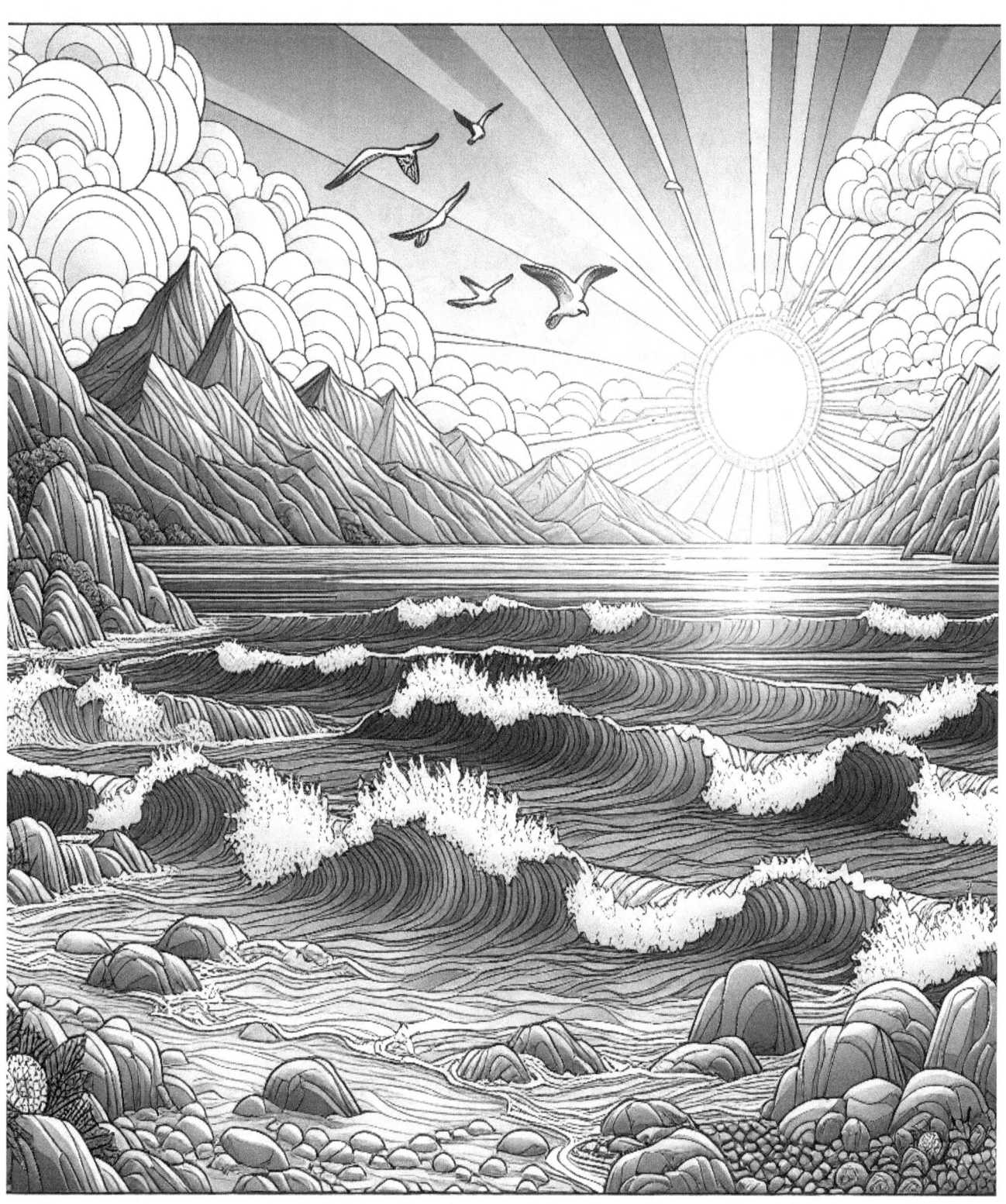

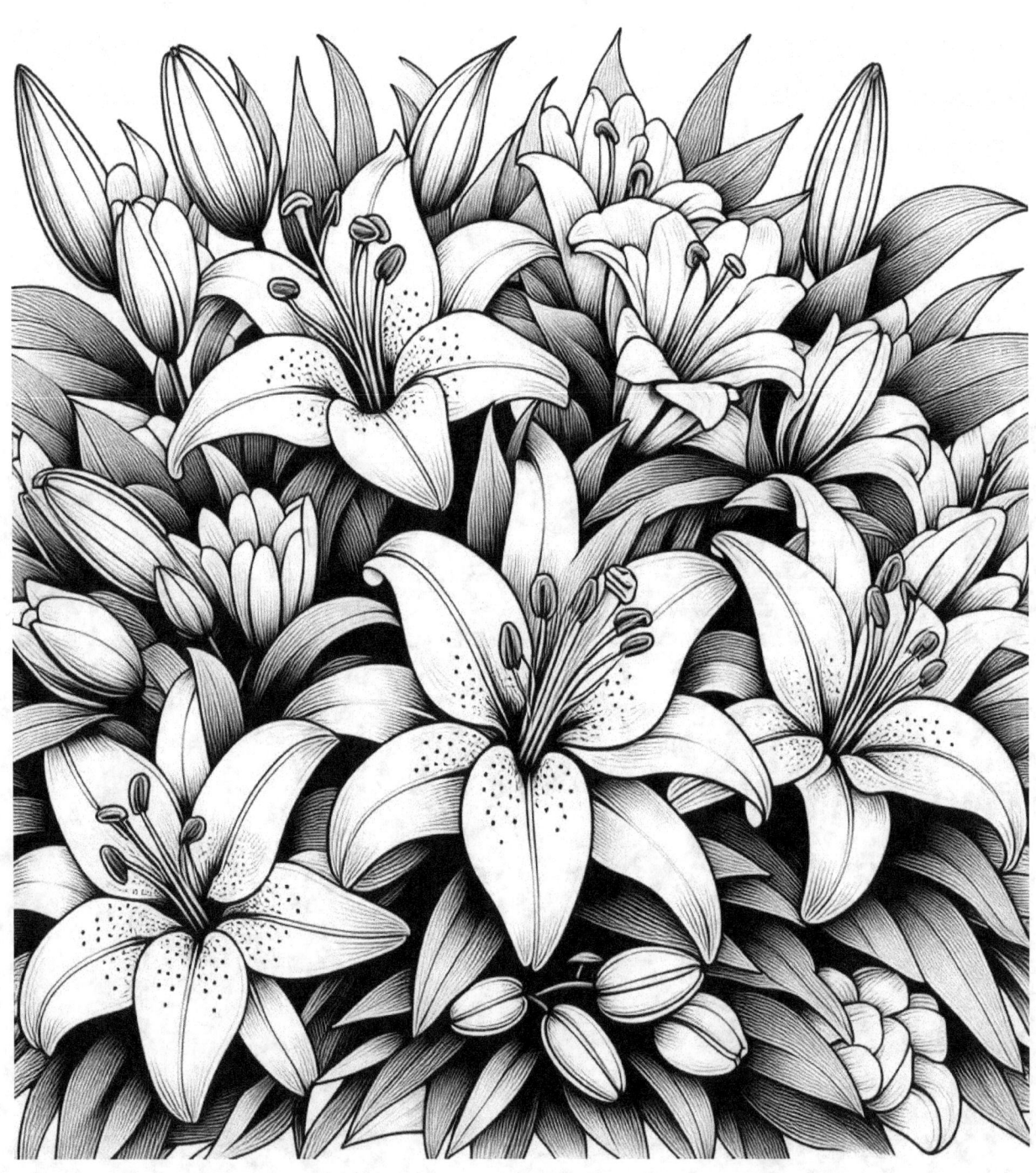

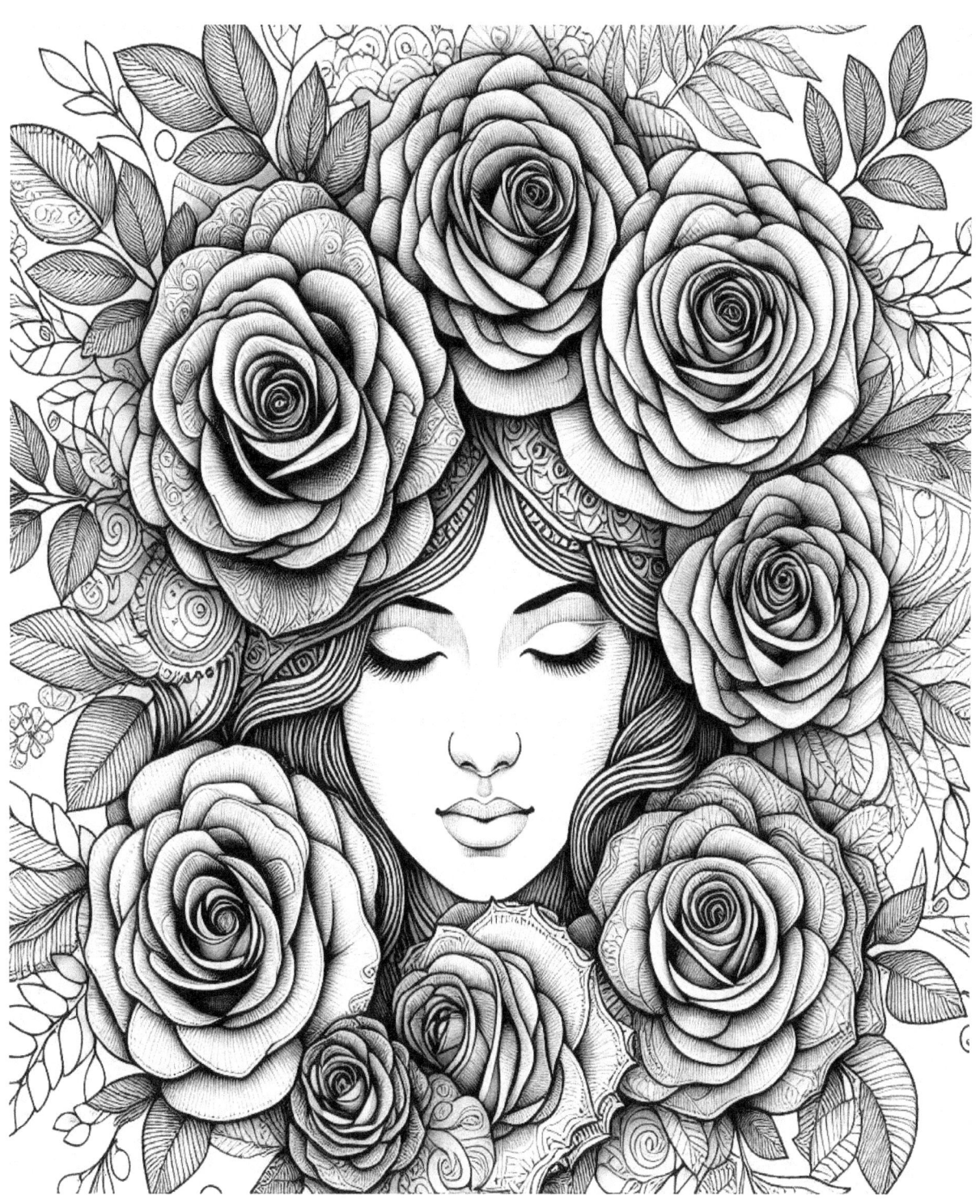

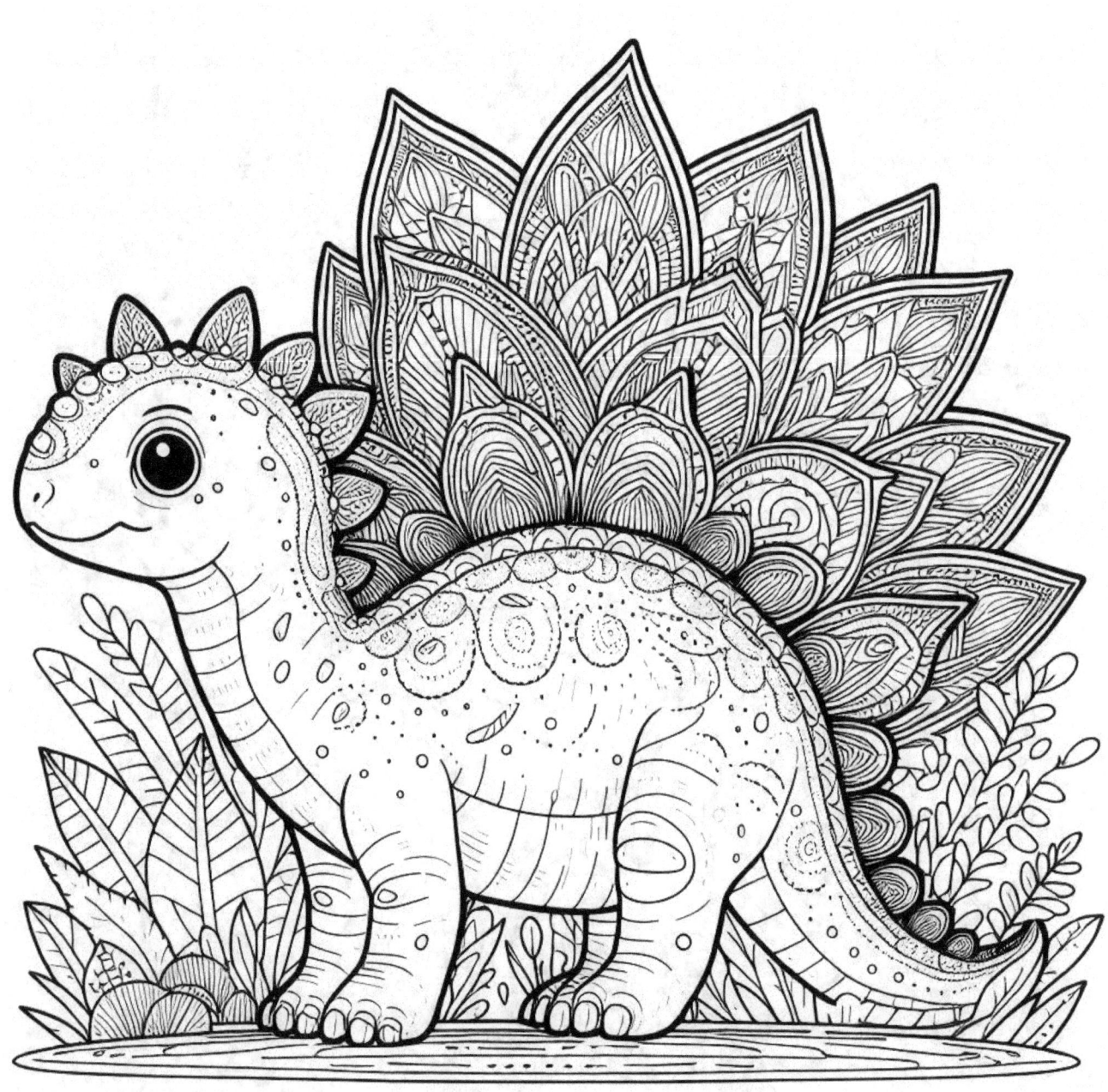

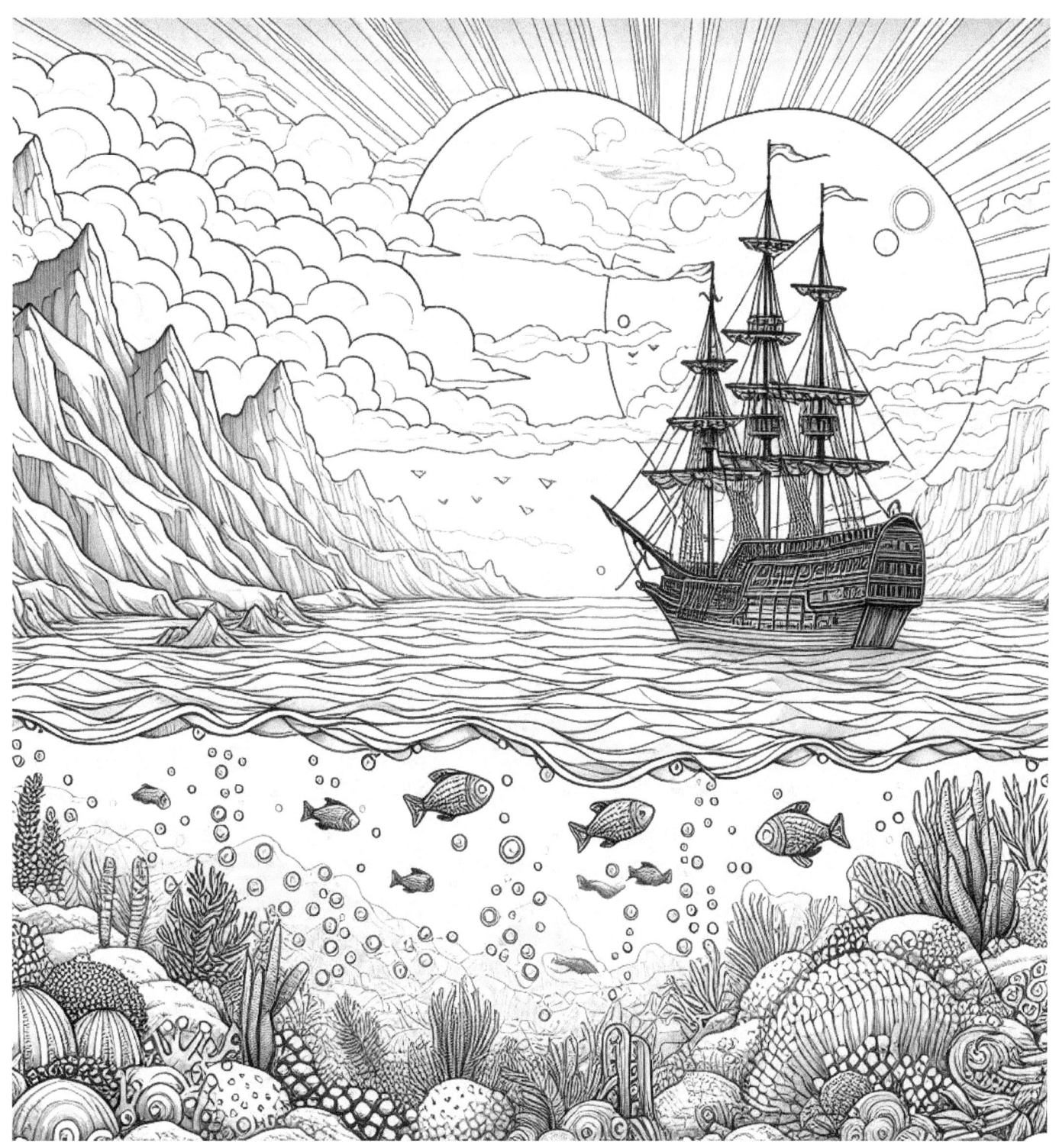

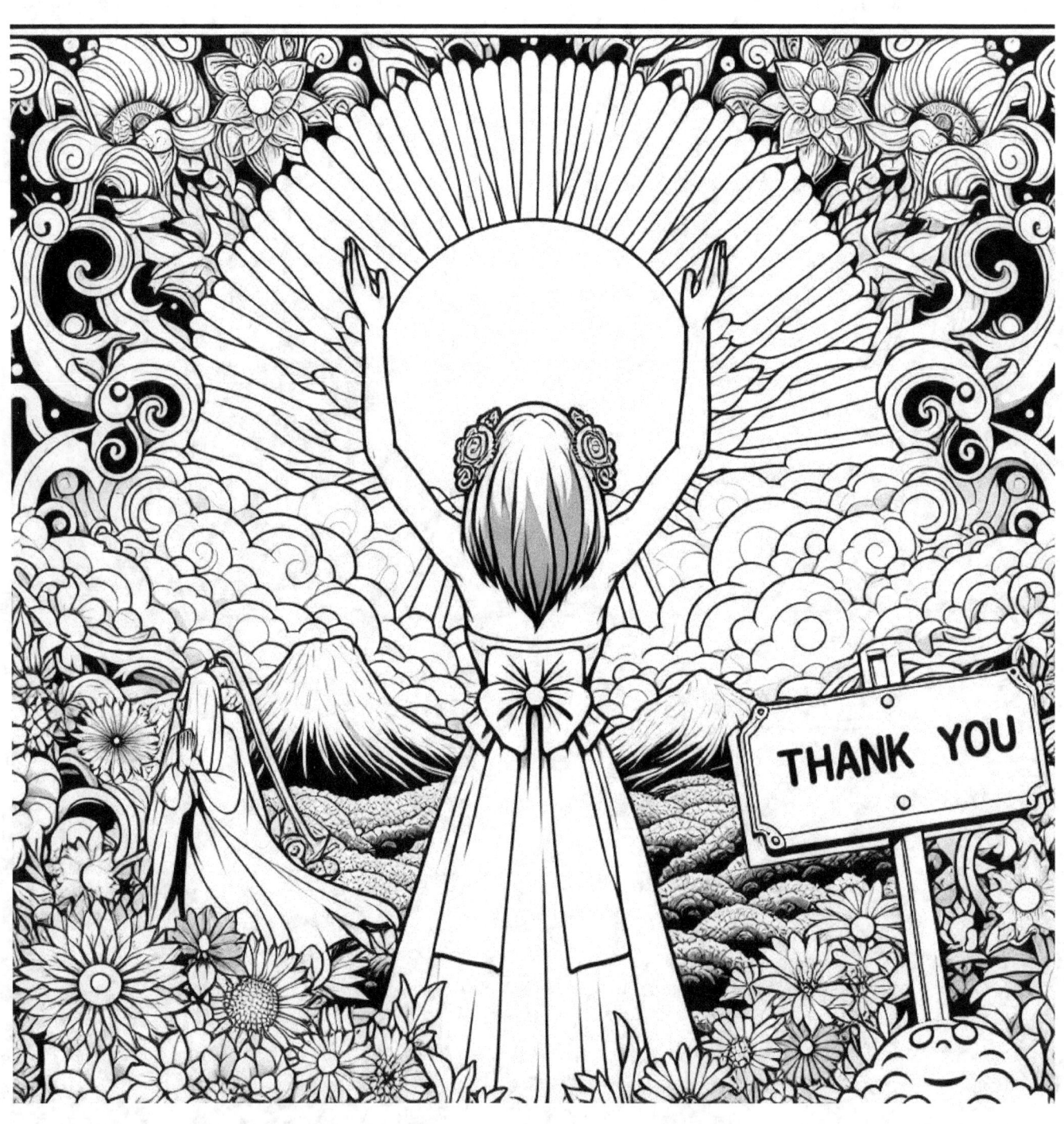

May this book be just the beginning of your artistic journey! Move forward with confidence and pride in every stroke of color you leave on these pages. Always remember that each artwork is unique and reflects your innate creativity and talent. Dare to explore and develop your artistic skills even further! The world is full of possibilities, so keep exploring, creating, and leaving your unique mark in everything you do!